Gentle Tugs

A Celebration of Life, Love, and Other Addictions

Janet K. Brennan

Published by Casa de Snapdragon Publishing LLC
A Traditional, Independent Publishing Company
MMX

Library of Congress Cataloging-in-Publication Data
Brennan, Janet K., 1947-
  Gentle tugs : a celebration of life, love, and other addictions / Janet K. Brennan.
     p. cm.
  "Guest poetry copyright Peggie Devan, Charles Ades Fishman, and Janet Yaeger"--T.p. verso.
  ISBN 978-0-9840530-7-0 (pbk.)
  I. Title.

PS3602.R4498G46 2010
811'.6--dc22

2010008733

20101111
Published by
Casa de Snapdragon Publishing LLC
Albuquerque, New Mexico

Printed in the United States of America

For my beloved father, Joseph F. Devan who passed through his window on August 5, 2009

Preface

This book was a pure joy in the writing. I feel that it is my composition on life and the many facets of its complex puzzle. I am hoping to convey to my readers that all of life is a Tarantella and must be danced to the fullest in order to understand the journey.

Gentle Tugs is a celebration of life!

I want to extend a special thank you to Peggie Devan for allowing me to publish three of her most exceptional poems dealing with celebration and holidays; Charles Adés Fishman, thank you for your glorious poem *In My Grandpa's Shoes* a celebration of family; and Janet Yaeger for her inclusion of *The Family Album*.

Special gratis goes to my mentor and friend, Louie Levy, Peace Poet.

The wonderful writing of the following poets whose work has inspired me:

> Lynn Strongin –British Columbia, Canada
> Maya Angelou - USA
> Charles Adés Fishman –New York, USA
> Katriona Wallace- Oslo, Norway
> John Newlin – California, USA

And of course, my loving husband, editor, and friend, Art.

The Family Album

Janet Yaeger

Like a haunting of my memory, my ghosts of yesterday
Fill my head with visions that I thought I'd put away.
As I walk through dusty cobwebs in the attic of my mind,
I search through trunks of memory, not sure what I will find.

Little bits of yesterday are at my fingertips,
Scraps of fabric of my life, somehow I can't resist
The strong temptation to explore my crowded memory
And look at snippets of my life, which have been left for me.

I see my life before me, like an album opened wide,
From infancy to grownup, my family at my side.
I see myself transforming to a woman from a girl,
As I learn from others and take my place in this world.

I continue turning pages in the album of my life,
I see my life unfolding as I now become a wife.
Children quickly follow and I see them grow.
All too soon, they're grownup, before I even know.

I turn more pages as I see my life continue on,
Page after page of images, each memory more strong.
But, as I near the last page of the album, I can see
Pages are not filled up, there are still some empty.

I put the album back into my trunk of memories
I close the lid, and lock the lock, and shake dust off of me.
I walk back through the cobwebs in the attic of my mind,

Knowing I'll be back some day to see what I can find.

Gentle Tugs

Most nights I sit
watching a perfect sun
set over the mesa- wide,
dreaming of a place, new
to hang my hat
should I wander from this place
to greener pastures by the sea.
A lake with Loons.
How I love Loons!

Pattering rain on a tin-roof;
snow frosting a window, north.

My reverie ended,
"We're here"
Children, grandchildren and pets,
passing hugs,
telling jokes,
ice-cold drinks,
firing the grill.
Laughter
through old Bryce Canyon.
Gentle tugs.
"Where is your hat, Gram?"
A hearty reply…
"Right where it belongs, love
Right where it belongs."

Janet K. Brennan

Prelude

Bath water warm, matching her life,
she slips from beneath
white gossamer
into the bubbly Badedas.
Filling the ceramic,
the best time of the day.
Water 'neath her chin
as it kisses her breasts.
Seduction complete!
Immersed in a cocktail- perfumed,
contented sighs escape,
as the door flies open.

Two intruders.
One with a bottle, the other a doll.
"Not now, kids, Mum is off on a cloud."

Kneeling, gazing at her belly-swollen,

"Make him kick, mum, please!"

Sweet sigh-curtain's up.
Silence, the first all day,
warm hands envelop her belly,
soft as her gentle laugh.

"Just one time and then off you go!"

They wait.
Suddenly, a quick flutter, stutter.
Baby wakes
to join the family just beyond his touch.
Four little hands,

pressed to front and sides,
as siblings laugh with joy.

"What is he doing, Mum? Is he kicking?
Is he all right?"

"Oh yes, luv-bugs, he is fine.
He is eager to join us.
He is simply giving us gentle tugs…

Just a few gentle tugs!"

Janet K. Brennan

Encantations in Song

Her laughter fills the universe.
And tho i try,
i can not fly
so high
or touch her wings
as she soars the sky.

Sweet child of conjure!
Little girl –woman;
encantations-transfiguration!

Curls dark, upon her face,
body strong, enchanted;
sweet mother's daughter,
sings for us and God.
Angels, her choir, friends
who visit her dreams,
enfolding in their watch,
playing when she morphs
 to cat Amos.
They dance with crickets
'neath a Cheshire-moon,
waking with tit-mouse
when the last star
fades from her heaven.

Mother's daughter, sweet sorceress.
Growing to a woman.
And tho i try,
i can not fly
or touch her wings
when she soars
so high.

Her mother's flower,
sweet Wizards
throw care to the wind,
spreading seeds
through wild meadows.
And tho i try
i can not fly,
or touch their wings
when they soar
so high.

For she, her mother's flower,
and i,
although i try,
to fly so high
and touch the sky
am yet
her mother's roots.

Janet K. Brennan

Amongst Sweet Rose and Willow

Laughing...
She lay amongst Foxglove
where light, eternal
falls upon her breasts, silken;
dreaming of a mid-day sun
that she may dance.
~~

She cries
under the willow-weep
for all
who gaze on distant stars.
For life is naught
but this beautiful day!
~~

Her rose stem, thorns
yet, fears not pain
that has forged a tired soul,
swiftly gilding its heart.
She does not bleed!
~~

A dance, macabre
on a moonless night.
Stumbling on ghosts buried,
preaching of truths, hidden.
She has battled her darkest hour
and won the war!
~~

Armor tested
with stamp eternal,
she sleeps upon thistle,
knowing only the moment;
mourning those
who gaze upon distant stars,
never learning to lie
amongst sweet-rose and willow.

Janet K. Brennan

Erin Elizabeth

Wind, tousled,
honey brown hair,
enshrouding
her nakedness.
She runs down the hill.
Chubby legs,
leaping and dancing,
reveling in raw pleasure
of wind against skin.

> Shallow water,
> enveloping her, baby soft,
> she splashes, ecstasy!
> Once, stopping
> to gaze at her reflection
> changing
> in ripples of blue,
> . . . she wonders . . .

Incarnation. . . jubilation!
Absolute rapture!
Sweet abandon!
Accepting joy
in physical delights
made possible
by the innocence of
her neonate soul . . .

A Rose Hiding

She is but a rose, hiding
washed in colors, pink.
Petals . . .
Amongst Baby's Breath
White.
Buried in a garden, deep
where lovelies do proclaim
their beauty bare.
She hides . . .
where none can see
through flowers, bold.
Her thorns, small,
fragrance, sweet.
Hidden by choice
in the shade of her own
that she may sing
in a gentle voice
for only God to hear.

Janet K. Brennan

Last Night's Dream

Dusty road running, ghost-flower riddled
Peeping from cracks

Steps, unguarded, boulders, ripe-moss
Inconsiderately placed - ~~narrows
 to a one horse trail

Falling upon prickly, forgotten remnants
from yesterday's garden
I give thanks to Deus – my soul unbroken
I rise!

I Am A Willow

.....I am a Willow
Winds, foraging
my branches . . . feathers
stretching my soul
kissing the dampness
of the cold ground

bending, swaying
bowing, praying
thanking, that although
the tempest wild
.....I am a Willow~~

Atahsaia: Catching Fireflies[1]

He fades on this moonlit walk, shrinking violet
through fields of fire flies, before they leave
His footsteps soft through cutter grass
sharp against ghost legs, jar in hand,
disappearing-reappearing
Black curls cropped above sage bush, he reaches
to catch the flash moving in and out of his life,
capturing it in his lightning bug jail
A whoop and a holler, he heads through the meadow,
shoulder deep in Luna's light; he blinks away the moment
lest she memorize his soul
Howling a mournful song, he takes her lightness
to the Rio in water deep and dark for a swift ride
to nowhere; for he hides deep in his meadow
while fading on this moonlit walk, a shrinking violet
through fields of lightning bugs and cutter grass
on this last night of summer

---

[1] *Atahsaia is the Zuni Demon of the night who has been known to hide behind rocks and sage brush during the day . There is also a deep metaphor in this poem.*

11

Janet K. Brennan

The Cultured Pearl

Hiking her skirt above her knees, she sits,
a pearl of wisdom, legs dimpled.
She likes what she sees. He wonders.
Did she do this just for him?
Edging her legs, tanned, toned,
he pretends not to notice .
His manhood tested, he made the grade!

Sipping her drink, she smiles at the waiter.
Nice eyes…sweet young thing.
She winks as he brings her another
double with a twist. She likes the twist!

Laughing at his jokes,
touching his hand, rubbing that finger,
wedding band gone for a while.
White where the sun never reaches,
an indentation forever there .
Hers, replaced by a cultured pearl
when her own went missing
in the back of his truck.
He smiles at her giggles and jiggles,
as the skirt slips higher.

Did he notice? Did he enjoy?

She is in love with love; he is in love with her;
yet they both know, all that glitters…

The Sage

She was here, our Margarita.
Flew in with the canyon winds.
We welcomed her.
We danced
upon the desert sands-barefoot
late at night.
Her wisdom told us to be brave.
We would see the sun
even though the night black
and wrought with demons.
.

She cried with us.
Swallowed our tears whole into her own.
Found joy
in the smallest wildflower
growing amongst rocky cracks;
its perfume sweeter for the toil.
Embracing
beauty in the hidden grace
of yet the darkest soul,
knowing light bounds.
.

We prayed with her.
Family incantations.
We were hers and she ours
in the early morning hours
when they said she had gone home.
And we knew
that none such as she
had ever graced this earth
nor loved God more
quite like our Margarita.

Janet K. Brennan

The Shrine

His eyes absorb,
she gazes.
Life s reflection;
their temple of dreams.
Quick tousle of hair,
a peck on her cheek,
he is won by a sideways glance.
All these years. . .
when the babes were young;
the pets new, and laughter
bounced down halls,
leaving quiet shadows
behind gilded frames.
Now, only cat Amos knows
their secret sounds.
Yesterday, today.
for time is not
in their temple of dreams.
Though their dance a bit slower,
these blessed days shorter,
his eyes absorb
a sideways glance, and

they waltz.

Unspoken Words

Your lips-soft
brush my hair, tangled.

     You move, slowly

          to rest upon my cheek,

               nibbling my ear...whispering.

To the tip of my nose,
     a slight hesitation.
          Down to my lips,
               enveloping mine, deep.

Not a word did you speak.
Yet, everything said
I could ever want to hear.

Janet K. Brennan

Apron Pockets

Her prayer beads worn
She waits just for Him
Apron pockets-a cross
To remind not to sin
.

Brothers, sisters are gone
She lived and has learned
All this time on the earth
Heaven she 's earned
.

Old hands shake with age
Her eye sight grows dim
She is ready to go
On a prayer and a whim
.

When the back door flies open
It too, weathered and worn
What is happening outside?
It must be a storm!
.

Oh no, not the wind
But her granddaughter here
A fall in the garden
Needs sweet Grammy cheer!
.

Then up on her lap
It does not take long
A little girl smile
Mixed with dear grandma song
.

So glad you are here, Gram
I' m all better, you see?
My, perhaps one more lesson
Between God and me

Her old prayer beads worn
Today a bit stronger
Still lessons to learn
Sorry, Lord
I need a bit longer!

Janet K. Brennan

A Midnight Play on Words

Sleep eludes her this night
Feet jump 'neath the quilt
As the clock ticks away
Lucid moments of guilt

As the mind travels on

Warm baths and softball
Ballet and art class
Vermouth bitter-sweet
In a half filled glass

Cat Amos snuggles close
Collie on the floor
Lord, did she remember
To lock the front door?

Did she kiss them, sweet dreams
Graced with a smile?
"Not to worry my loves,
Daddy's gone for a while"

And the mind travels on

Did she mail that last bill?
Will it get there on time?
Just a few days late
They said it was fine

Gentle tugs on her pillow
A kiss on her cheek
As a new day is born
The start of a week

Cat Amos purrs heavy
The collie wants out
Her children's gay laughter
Is what life's about

A new day begins
Heart's sweet, gentle song
And waits for the night
When the mind wanders on

And waits for the night
When the mind wanders on

Janet K. Brennan

Passiflora

You place upon my limbs
Roses, black,
soaked in passion-breath,
tender, as you move upon me.

Passiflora

This tango, bittersweet,
for there are thorns
amongst the loveliest.
This dance of pain and flame,
rhythm...exquisite,
one and the same.
Your lips inside.

Passiflora

The Morphing of Stillwater

Swells crash, my Paradisio,
turning –churning-crushing,
memories
ground to powder white.
Satin-soft
slipping between my toes
and moving beneath my feet;
the shore alive,
my balance shaken to the core.

Were you there?
I felt your laughter deep
as we caught the water's edge,
carrying dreams
from your world to mine
while sea birds sang
the song of life.
My old ones out of tune;
not forgotten, simply melting
as I move into the turning tide.

Shell sublime held tight in my hand,
a secret within.
White from burning sun.
Fragile, cracks open for Doves to fly
I watched them fly!

Janet K. Brennan

A Stronger Grace

Mourning whispers
watered down hues of gray pearl.
Sweet moment, quick
greeting yet another day,
though unwelcome guest.
She is gracious in her hosting.

Invitations never extended
~~~these days.

There is no partner in the dance!
Only shadows, gray in a box
stored under her bed.
Negatives of life . . . shared
when he sang only for her
...not for God.
Loving arms, no more
her cloak in the storm.
Her captain, missing,
taking laughter with him.
She sails her ship alone.

Pray, each new day, a stronger grace,
that her soul-mate, gone
smile down on her,
knowing how resilient- his flower,
though bent upon the ground
waiting to bloom again.

~~~For she will bloom!
As she wanders through life
a stronger grace ...
Accepting only sacred vows,
now cast to heaven

Leaving paths through the stars
for her to follow
and dance with him again
when it is her time.

Janet K. Brennan

Sweet Clover

Unguarded,
chains cut.

You slipped into my heart
stepping past my watch.

Laying sweet clover at my feet,
bathing them in myrrh.
Smiling behind stories

never-ending.

Scheherazade's tale, sweet exchange.
Your kiss for my soul.
In a moment unguarded reveals an ending…

Stealing away into a thousand and one
taking my heart, scattering my chains
among sweet clover…

Confessions of a Soulmate

Once
in another world, timeless
~~ we loved
emotions, feelings
completion .
Moving into each other,
creating one soul...sharing
joy, grace, sorrow,
ah, passion-lust!
We could not feel
 Longing to touch
Solutions of incarnation.

Through lightness, we moved
searching ~~

Completion, wholeness, signs.
~~ Praying to be found.

Two stars,
our paths crossed,
... and we knew!

Janet K. Brennan

The Willow

My beautiful Desert Willow,
ravaged by summer hail.
Leaves stripped from its tender branches.
Cuts sliced into its trunk.
Bent and broken from strong winds.
It will not survive . . . I am sure.

Time and season have mercifully
brought buds to its bare branches.
Tender, green now covers what was
white and torn.
Erect it stands, with its limbs reaching
eagerly for the sun.

My beautiful Desert Willow.
Once ravaged by summer hail.
Now sways accommodatingly in the winds.
Proudly displaying
its hard earned foliage.
It will survive . . I am sure!

My Willow is all accepting.
Without sorrow, it sheds its leaves.
It waits, and sleeps and remembers,
that in dormancy lays its renewal,
and strength to blossom again.

When it is time!

Treasures in a Coffee Can

Eyes wide, she gathers
Packs away.
Protecting her hoard
for a cold winter's day.

Sunflowers, tattered
Peaches dripping, now soft
An old brown nut
from last year's crop.

Chrysanthemums, dried
An old corn stalk.
Dandelions, gold
plucked from lava rock.

Sour berries, dried cherries
in a mini pie pan.
Treasured selections
placed in a blue coffee can.

Happy meal trinkets
rest on the pile
with a lock of brown hair
now gone for a while.

I'll save them for keeping
until the next spring
They are all so lovely
won't throw away a thing!

My garden so precious
to a true old soul
One would never imagine
just five years old!

Janet K. Brennan

Singin' and Dancin'

Momma, I'm dancin'.
I take wing across
the highest peaks
painting my image wholly
in pastel clouds, pink
here-gone,
a gift for your eyes only.

Momma, I'm singin'.
You heard me in the dawn.
A robin on your window's ledge
Missing naught your touch
for your spirit warms me
with your love.
Wrapping around my soul
you are here, each time you rise.
For time is not
when standing in a higher place.

Feel my joy!
Mourning is but for yourself.
I am not gone, simply there!
Oh, think, sweet Momma!
You must know
what choir we make
when we sing and dance together!

Concerto at Longboat

My place perfect, I am bound
to sit on Longboat Shore.
Sugar covers my toes
as fluffy winged seraphim
dive for jewels, encrusted
diamonds in a late-day- glow.

Deities whisper watery hues purple
across pastel heavens,
as a tangerine diva sinks with majesty
into a sea of gold…
Bravissimo!

Lord Maestro bows one last time.
Critique perfect
as the Night Heron sings its first.
The curtain falls,
and I in my front row seat!

The following five poems were written by:

- *My sister, Peggie Devan. Her 3 poems deal with one of the most important aspects of a full life…celebration*
- *Charles Adés Fishman, a Pulitizer Prize Nominee wrote* **In His Granpa's Shoes**,
- *And Janet Yaeger sums up the true message and essence of this book with* **The Family Album**.

Thanks so much, Peg, Janet, and Charles!

Masquerade

Peggie Devan

Donning the mask on All Hallows' Eve rise
"Who are you?" he asks
For it is a surprise

A giggle is heard behind the unchanging face
"I am a songbird
Laden with grace"

"Then sing me your song brought forth from your heart
To treasure for life-long,
To keep when we part"

"My songs are for others and often for me,
For friends and my lovers,
Who knows ... perhaps thee?"

"But, if I should sing unmasked from my heart
A disguise I must bring
To wear when we part."

"Well, tonight should be fun and only a game
To sojourn as one,
Yet, remain the same"

"So, 'tis best left masked; to playfully retreat
And never to ask
Is this a trick or a treat?"

Ah, now the sun raises the Masquerade ends
There are no surprises
They still remain friends.

Traditionas...Generations

Peggie Devan

Turkey vapors rise dancing with plies' and with twirls
The children play...prancing...The boys chasing the girls

Mixed aromas of mince pie filters through pumpkin...cooling
"Nicky kissed me"...a fake cry...A faint smile proves she's fooling

Mmm... the sage and the thyme envelops the bread stuffing
The young teens rap with rhyme and a new rhythm called shuffling

Potatoes glazed with sweetness...pearl onions laced with butter
The young couple share their likeness, words of love they softly utter

New England breads, ahh... now warm... cinnamon raisin scents the air
Oh, their marriage now reformed has once again found its flair

The hues of fall flowers embrace the feast's table
The old folks rock for hours absorbing life as they are able

The repast now prepared...the wine poured to cheer
And those gathered will share, wishing you,

"Happy Thanksgiving" this year

In His Granpa's Shoes

Charles Adés Fishman
To Jake Hunter Esposito

The shoes are far too big,
but he half manages to walk
in them — shuffling and stumbling
like the greatgrandpapa he remembers.

I think the shoes are the right size
for him   and should stay unlaced,
not stowed away in the dark Atlantis
of our hall closet,

so this child may discover the path
imagination takes: no slight-of-hand
but the fancy footwork of vision.

In Grandpa's shoes, he will lift off
from this hate-trodden planet,
astronaut   of unhoped for grace.

While Visions of My Sister Danced in My Head

Peggie Devan

With the Christmas moon rising o'er my New Hampshire dream
We lay near the window in a silver moon beam

Remember past Christmases unable to slumber
We watched with excitement, 'is Santa near' we would wonder

We reminisced on our youth, so pure and believing
We'd listened for Santa, "It's our wishes he's leaving?"

My eyes wide with fright when you sent me to sneak
Down the stairs stepping lightly, 'round the corner I peeked

Oh yes, they were there, displayed under the tree
Through dimly lit boughs, crafted for you and me

No secrets were spoiled despite "pinky swear",
"Jan, he has not yet come" I lied with great flair

Visions danced in our heads while we laughed at our youth
The stories, some differ, doesn't matter the truth

So this year we send greetings to you with our smiles
"Merry Christmas, Good Tidings, Love and Light 'cross the miles"

Janet K. Brennan

The Family Album
Janet Yaeger

Like a haunting of my memory, my ghosts of yesterday
Fill my head with visions that I thought I'd put away.
As I walk through dusty cobwebs in the attic of my mind,
I search through trunks of memory, not sure what I will find.

Little bits of yesterday are at my fingertips,
Scraps of fabric of my life, somehow I can't resist
The strong temptation to explore my crowded memory
And look at snippets of my life, which have been left for me.

I see my life before me, like an album opened wide,
From infancy to grownup, my family at my side.
I see myself transforming to a woman from a girl,
As I learn from others and take my place in this world.

I continue turning pages in the album of my life,
I see my life unfolding as I now become a wife.
Children quickly follow and I see them grow.
All too soon, they're grownup, before I even know.

I turn more pages as I see my life continue on,
Page after page of images, each memory more strong.
But, as I near the last page of the album, I can see
Pages are not filled up, there are still some empty.

I put the album back into my trunk of memories
I close the lid, and lock the lock, and shake dust off of me.
I walk back through the cobwebs in the attic of my mind,
Knowing I'll be back some day to see what I can find.

Just One More Time

Music fills my parlor
as the last rays of a golden sun
slip through tiny shades of a
forgotten yesterday,
just one more time.
.
Only the crescent moon eavesdrops
as it wanders through my window,
shining upon your face,
just one more time.
.
Arms reach, lifting my soul
from tired, weathered places.
Lips brush my cheek,
soft from my evening wash.

       Off we go!
.
Twirling 'round the floor,
as we do each night
in steps . . . synchronized.
Our melody, cherished
from your mouth to mine
as your face burrows deep
into my tousled locks . . .
.
Breath, sweet tickles my ear
as you whisper
"Just one more time, my dear?"
Cheek on cheek
we dance the dance of life,
just one more time!

Janet K. Brennan

Memories of Dinner on the Adige

Sumptuous dinner, late.
Ingesting what I recognized
French cognac, watered down.
. . .One more chapter.

Sliding the case, golden .
Secretly inhaling its contents
old tobacco, spice, long gone
… I miss it.

Ducks in a moat
slide down crevices, antique
in this city by the Adige.
Castelvecchio, moss covered
beckons in the dank, river- night.
…
 Gathered treasures.

That last amber swig,
fiery hidden vice, rendering
vulnerable to cobblestones
that separate me from my hotel.

Rumbling autobus.
Companions smoke and dust.
Drown the edge
of my last drink.

"Lira for my sick child, Signora?"

Aspirin in pockets.
Impatience on my breath.
Forgotten gratuities, placed
into her hand, trembling.
I need to move on.

Janet K. Brennan

Lime Tree Bay

As soft sleepy sighs of bay
kiss a rocky shore,
I am adrift
between the seas
and Caribbean breeze .
Only the horizon
gives glimpse
to God's infinity.
Hemingway's paradisio,
one with sea and sky.
My life, the raft on a gentle wave,
...carries me on.
Did Ernest dream of such?
This song of blue and key lime,
...endless time
...forever days
exist simply to insult
what I knew before now.
And, I ask. . . . .
How can I turn home?

Surrendering to the Song

Ivory keys
stretch my night,
hiding from sleep   .
as my fingers dance
~~~andante,
caressing each chord
with passionate delight.
Transforming.
Carrying me to divine
as wood cotton
caught in a midnight wind.
~

Alone with the moon,
… a frequent lover
visits,
lighting the pages
through a melody, deep
until my soul
surrenders to the song.

Mi' Pianissimo, we are one.
A musical landscape.
 Symphony…
as we sail away
on a midnight song.

Janet K. Brennan

Reflections of Kate

Standing before the mirror
She cannot help but sigh
What small pubescent body
Who can I be and why?

      Not wise, too young they tell her
      Yet wisdom knows its host
      She smiles, she cries, she questions
      Those wizards she loves most

When will this small assembly
Match that which is so whole
With wings spread wide she ponders
Reflections of the soul

Nicholas Laughed in His Sleep

Nicholas laughed in his sleep last night.
Ol' Grandfather just chimed three.
I slipped down the hall, peeked 'round his door.
A mother's heart needed to see.

Asleep in his bed
With his quilts 'round his head.
Army Teddy clutched under his arm.
A smile on his face as he traveled through space.
With ol' teddy to keep him from harm.

His basketball hoop barely hung on his wall.
His wrestler guys played in the dark.
At the foot of his bed was his baseball cap- red.
An old wooden bat from the park.

His cars and his trucks all lined in a row.
Awaiting the morning's big race.
His Superman night-light casting a glow
On his angel sweet, nine-year-old face.

Yes, Nicholas laughed in his dreams, last night.
Keeping beat with ol' Grandfather's chime.
As I kicked at a sock and a petrified rock.
All was right in his world and mine!

The Pirate

Blond haired thief
That scallywag. . .
Leaving with more
than he brought
to my earthly lair
Eyes blue, voice brave
He dances through the stars
while I sleep, dreaming
Kiss soft as feather-down
He smiles and winks
… knowing
that he has all that is mine
… to give
And, I will see him into
the night

For Peyton Alexander

Prayer for Mother

Offer her Your gentle hand
As she begins this day
Shower her with loving grace
In each and every way
Send choirs of angels chorusing
Oh! Dance in your pure light
And when it's time to go to bed
Please
Kiss my Mum goodnight

Her Glorious Song

Her voice,
suddenly here.
Not there yesterday.
Yet, today she sings !

Sweet child,
vibrato strong,
heard in Heaven
a sent- kiss.

Oh, the power of song!
Far greater than all.
This gift
through life, will carry
into the next,
knowing
from whence it came.

She gives prayer
each time she sings.
That she may share
her thanks to God.

Oh, thank you, God!
She has this day
that You may hear
her glorious song . . .

Janet K. Brennan

April Soft

An angel lit upon her cheek
and kissed a dimple bold.
Then scurried off to find her heart,
encasing it with gold.

It wove a thread of shiny silk
and laced with shining light.
All through her soul for all to see,
her essence…diamond bright.

Her hands were next and they were made
of Angels' dust, quite rare.
All mixed with love and April- soft,
for they were meant to care.

For Peg

Cartwheels on the Lawn

We grew together, the three of us,
the way sisters always do.
Sharing rooms and whispering dreams,
loving as we grew.

Giggles and laughter late at night.
Waking on Christmas at dawn.
Trips to the lake on the Fourth of July.
Cartwheels on the lawn.

Secrets we told about each of our loves.
Fables to please Mom and Dad.
Tears and heartbreak and plans gone askew.
Every new home we had.

Though we are different,
we learned from those differences,
sharing just keeps going on.
And I say little sisters, life with you in it.
is like cartwheels on the lawn!

For my two sisters, Peg and Patricia

Janet K. Brennan

A Moment with Infinity

I lie upon this mantel verdant wealth,
stroking tendrils, roots buried deep,
dreaming the day I will not be,
for I am.
Stained fingers, mingled with life-blood
throughout veins stretching a soul
until it has reached the highest branch
that almost shades.
Syncopated dance, glimmer of time- stilled.
Praying to join in spider-weave-threads,
perfect bound;
falling
from limb to limb, sweet hierarchy
of thought
linking ground to sky to
universal God and beyond.

Destiny, Said Venus to Mars

The groan of another day.
She is in her place
watching wind- born- blossoms
in their journey to nowhere.
She catches them, lets them go.
Inhaling sweet, those flowers,
sprinkled with perfume from Eros,
while you fly through your largest dream
pursuing destiny.
She teaches, you stagger,
blinded by the dust
from her heart swept clean.
Still you moan another day
not comprehending why
you love her so

even though
you knew before you came.

Janet K. Brennan

A Million Flecks of Light

Pierce heaven, glistening,
blinding my eyes to truths
buried 'neath warm sands .
Will time create wrinkles,
or massage to liquid- silk?
As shells in a sea of storms
tumble to shore at high tide,
shattered by whispers, harsh
and turned to powder.
Years move on.
.
Luna plays hide and seek
on this night of nights.
Beckoning sweet surrender.
dancing between storms;
juggling a million flecks of light.

     And I wonder. . .

He walked on water,
can he rise above transgressions of the heart?

Will you love me forever?
Clouds sweep across an imaginarium
illusive, intrusive.
Forever is now!
As a million flecks of light
pierce heavens, glistening-bouncing,
blinding my eyes to truths
that shatter as crushed shells
carried to shore on a midnight tide.
.
     Luna touches her face and smiles.

Weathervane

Among dreams
I saw,
though my eyes pressed in sleep.
I felt a child, dancing in meadows.
Blessed abundance!
Posies chanting a destiny to Wind-Gods
beckoning me down paths without signs.
Mileage etched
deep within an ageless face.
And when I fell beneath a starless sky,
my body prone in universal bliss,
I prayed for wizardries
that I may rise above meadows, a feather
floating above wildflowers bowing
to life' s uncharted storm.
I felt my being lift.
Navigator,
as I watch the Wind-Gods laugh.

If in dreams, then so in life!

Janet K. Brennan

Tomorrow's Parade

Strike up the band!
My instrument tuned.
I the master, my master.
.

O, when will I learn?
.

My costume starched, threadbare.
Sheet music stained, pages torn
from practicing unto the night,
never getting it right!
Though my symphony where
it needs to be.
.

I cry-the stage so high.
Front row, forever away.
Faces dim, the lights too bright.
How I wish that I could see
smiles in my own gig!
.

Feet too slow, a stumble bum.
The pitch goes high for the rise.
Pride great, no lessons learned
from the mended threads
of my costume, starched.
.

Pray! When will I learn?
.

Strike up the band!
Quick click of the heels
and off to Oz I fly.
The distance far, having all I need

to laugh in tonight's dreams;
march in tomorrow's parade.
Never giving a care if I get it right.
For my symphony's where
it needs to be.

Janet K. Brennan

The Drum Master

She cries for her lost.
Echoing through canyons, down hills,
as a wolf, yet a maiden - perhaps.
Through the night she calls,
beckoning.
My footsteps in hers, the same.
Through foothills 'neath a solstice moon.
I saw her once upon her knees,
rubbing dirt across her face,
turning tears to mud.
Her robe, danced with the wind
that bathed her sorrow and begged her soul.
.

I saw the vision in the early morning rain
as she stayed her place in the mist,
Quan Yin-the vision complete.
A small child, held close to her breast.
Its small face as brown as the Rio
in mid-winter flow,
when the mountains let loose
capping through the early morning to the wash.
For she cries for her lost,
and raises above the land her hand
in desperate hunger for a sign
that she will hold her loved one again,
when the drum master comes to take.

Wild Flowers Bleed

We stood in the field, fallow -flaxen.
Dried and cutting wounds deep.
As I am born.
For life holds pain with bliss.
.

Will you love me should I bleed?
Would you carry me to the hills
tho there be snow?
Sure we will leave seeds to heavy the clouds
that we may learn to find our way home.
Oh, will they heal ?
For I have run with the wind-born
and forgotten how to pray.
.

You said you would find me.
Your arms strong.
Whispering tales of a thousand and one
until I forgot what I was not.
You kissed my eyes
that I might not see the storm
as I lay hidden
Roses in Thornbush.
Yet,you knew and lifted.
Your promise with wings.
Taking me through fields fallow.
Cutting wounds deep as I am born.

Oh, will you love me should I bleed?

Janet K. Brennan

Footprints in the Snow

Oh, did you see them
turning white to red?
Hardly there!
Crimson whispered
as a winter flower,
popping through cold
Petals carried to God
She flies;
bent in the wind,
inhaling her time
Knowing that life is but
a sent kiss melting
in the morning sun.

Glory Flowers

What greater way to speak of love
than to stand upon the hill,
Olive branch ground to bits of gold,
offering naught but the hand that helps in the climb?
Strong...
destroying terror
without terrorizing the destroyer.

What better way to speak of mercy
than to take away pain of war?
Planting it as a bush of thorns
in the path that climbs.
Sweet challenge of transition!
Burning it with joy.
Inhaling its harmony - spice,
reminding that without peace, we can not play
nor love
or stroke another's flag, retaliation.
We remain as lions- cell captive
desiring freedom yet tripping over glory flowers;
destroyed only in winds of dissent.

What greater way to say life is wholly
than to stand upon the hill?
Olive branch ground to bits of gold.
Offering naught but the hand that helps in the climb,
whispering.

We have lost the battle of blood.
Yet, won the war of spirit.

Glory flowers!

Janet K. Brennan

The Waiting Game

They will play til dark'
flicker of street lights announce
time for dinner and home.
She waits.
Yet, shadows upon wooden slats
say she packs her dolls alone,
this time.
.

Losing herself in this game
before the next minute arrives
bringing salvation on a tray.
She prays for the peace that never comes,
as the baby cries for her breast,
not ready for the day.
.

The table leans right, sticky.
Could that be him,
the Gent with the rose?
They did not say flowers - he smiles
and sits with the blonde,
the one with the rings.
Maybe next time.
.

The pouring window.
A whiskey flag flies.
That time between five and six,
when the world sits back, glass in hand.
Sweet banner announces
to take that first drink.
Thank God, its time!.
.

Curtains drawn.
He will come with cakes.
He knows she loves tea,
a short visit, nice
when he brings the children.
They sit upon her knee
laughing into her folds of age.
.

Where has it gone?
.

Years engraved on her hands.
Maps that show more than she tells.
Sheets wet, changed in a minute.
The ticking of the clock.
The beating of her heart, one and the same.

While she waits.

Janet K. Brennan

Bowing Holy

Old Sandia glistens white,
bowing holy
on this early desert morn.
For snow has come in the night,
painting its hills and valleys
with sublime images
of Your glorious face.
.

Tiny green peeps through earth -brown
while my garden yet sleeps.
Life renewed, it calls
I am found!
Soon the Son will peek
a smile upon this day,
warming as I raise in praise.
.

You died, but never left
that I may
live and love.
For you are here with me
each moment of my days.
Oh Dear Lord!
What gift shall I give in return
but peace and joy
that surrounds my heart?
Is it grand enough ?
Wrapped in ribbons of grace
when e'er I breathe Your name.
For I bow low to Your Holy
this day and every day
in my desert place,

as Old Sandia glistens white,
and bows to Your Holy
on this most glorious day.

Janet K. Brennan

Memories of Monsoon, Last

Rain is coming, I can smell it,
pricking my skin with bits of sand
stolen with the wind' s offering.
A high desert commandment!
Good with bad, extremes of both.
Always the anticipation
that the sky will break.

.

I have been in the desert too long,
and yet, not long enough.

.

Sweet blend of Pinion and Sage
carried through passes
and down the mountain side.
I wait, we all wait,
inhaling memories of monsoon last
when high tide through arroyos
into the Rio Grande,
teased its boundaries of wild fruit
and bare cottons in the Bosque.

.

Hawks, mouths open,
wings folded in thankful prayer
for the quenching goodness
the spirits will bestow upon their thirsty .
They call, echoing through canyons
as they wing to higher ground .
And I too stand, face to the sky,
arms folded in prayer,
waiting.

Prayer in a Darkened Room

This road of cobbles,
bumping through feet, sore.
Boots without straps.
Soles, soul ripped raw.
I have traveled far, yet here I am,
careful not to step on cracks.
Oh, what do I learn each day I love?
Pray! What do I lose these days I live?
Indigent...
on this bejeweled path of tomorrows,
blinding to the knowledge
that all that glitters is not.
Your hand, larger than mine;
calloused by weight of lost prayers,
hidden well behind cursed pride.
My legs weaker as they move
closer to the bridge.
Sweet solicitations in prayer
for transcendence!
Will my fingers grasp Yours
when I fail to reach?
Will You cry if I do not try?
When I can not, will You rise?
Mesmerized by that crystal gaze.
My destiny undone!
For I know in the journey
my life is Yours, not mine.
Yet, can I surrender that part of me
that clings to the wonder of
what could have been?

Janet K. Brennan

As She Sang Amazing Grace

She sat on the divan
her lazy-day rest,
keeping beat with the floor boards,
Amazing Grace, her best.
.

As the damp ground beckoned,
she sang that day.
For tomorrows last sigh
but a night away.
.

"Bring them 'round," she cried.
"They are always on the go.
They don't come by often.
O I love them so!"
.

Only when mother lets them.
A few times, then gone.
Yet they loved her cozy
and her Amazing Grace song.
.

Angelic faces
Behind gilded frames.
School art on the fridge,
tiny slippers,childrens games.
.

Challenging them with questions
about God and Love.
She knew quite well;
her best friends from above.

They knew from Sunday School.
Each week, lessons taught.
Charity of the heart.
Yet, somehow they forgot.

.

Golden years surrendered
with baby bonnet-lace,
as she waited on her divan,
and sang Amazing Grace.

.

Now I sit on the sofa.
Amazing Grace, my mother's best.
Curling toes through woven quilts
in my lazy-day rest.

.

"Bring them 'round," I beg
"They are always on the go!
They don't stop by often
O I love them so!"

.

Only when daughter lets them.
A few times, then gone.
As the damp ground beckons,
and the hands of time move on.

Thank you, Leben…for putting this poem to music

Janet K. Brennan

Iona

For Katriona

And so
she sits beneath sage.
Her prayer for mercy, a friend.
Strength has carried to this mount,
and set her upon high places
moving silently along thorn bush trails,
dropping stones from pockets-deep
that she may return
should she lose her way by the setting sun.
.

Those kept as gold-dust
have turned to simple dreams
to keep her warm
should the night grow dark,
as when her Prince was gone.
.

Yet, she will rise to new days
whispering verse rehearsed
atop the peak.
And she will dance as a willow,
wind moving her branches,
carrying to sweet meadows below.

For she has climbed this mountain before,
and knows the way home

A Moment With Ravena

I will be your friend forever!
Words of truth-joy and love
dashed in a moment,
buried beneath ill thought.
The venom deep, we go our way.
Each one turning the same soil,
yet alone.
A moment gone, words of pain.

Once the arrow strikes
there is naught but to hold
the heart-wounded,
whispering words-unheard.
A prayer of hope carried close .
.
Enlighten my Lord!

For why we bend to the storm
and allow the darkest fray
to unleash that hidden sword
we carry neath our cloaks of grace.
Savage on those we love the most.
We crumble when they fall.
Wipe their tears of hurt, undone.
We are undone!
The truth hidden, intentions betrayed.
We can not make it right.
I will be your friend forever!
A lie from Satan s mouth?

Perhaps a misspent moment
dancing with Ravana.

Janet K. Brennan

Broken Lights

Silver puffs, the last in the pack
mingled
with whiskey, sweet fire.
His last swig as his world crushes
dreams to dust
melting ice in his last drink.
.

You can not tell her, she will cry,
and think that I am gone!
As soon as I clean up my gig
I ll be back in town.
.

Just one more drink,
with golden wings,
they will kiss the sky.
So many times he reached and failed
before he waved goodbye.
.

Alone he sings his lonesome song,
refrain, sweet refrain.
Chorus. Bridge- Chorus, echoes
through tunnels of life
as he flails beneath the weight
of his own hooded cape,

the one he hides
that none can see what lies beneath.
.

Now she stands in the door,
watching
as he smokes his last.

Broken lights, naked eyes.
It will be better this time,
rebirth!
And they will chant to the destinies
that hell is not eternal, and heaven waits.
.

No need to tell her, now she cries
and fears that he is gone.
As soon as he cleans up his gig,
he'll be back in town.

Janet K. Brennan

Dusting Cobwebs on a Winter Day

Scrub Jays clacking secrets,
as shadows of the day trip my mood,
begging gifts of pure release
in my journey through a late daydream.
Palmed feathers chanting of magic
whisper rumors of sun drenched shores,
water babies coming to visit
in a shallow seaweed bay.
.

Another world, it was!
.

Made better in the desert chill,
and jack frost mornings of tomorrow.
Burying my toes 'neath feather-down.
Remembering. . .
quilts of powder, white laced
with pearly shells and frothy tides
warmed by a tangerine gem
hung low beneath pillows- beige.

Impatient!

For that last hurrah into the sea.
Rose and blue tints remain,
melting across a dusky sky.
Creation at its best!
Leaving one thankful tear,
I remember and dream.
While winter birds sing through the night,
and snow hugs old watermelon high.
Winds skip through the canyon and sigh'

sweet dreams, my friend, sweet dreams.
Don't forget,
there is always next year.

Janet K. Brennan

Addiction

Bare necessity
O lamb of my waked dreams
Standing upon a ground that quakes
beneath the weight of your transgression
Hands that bleed from hanging too long
from the pity tree

.

      I can not save you

.

      But hope that in the climb
      you know which branches
      hold your weight

.

Yet, I am here
Needing you needing me
Stretched beyond wit or magic
Offering naught
but paste for your shattered image,
and a hand that will crumble
at sight of your next tear

Bella After Hours

Whispering down the night.
Streets empty, saved for crazies,
while she in her reverie
from whiskey- laced coke
sings for souls who are not there,
dances for lovers on a distant star
who flew home when she left the gig.

With nothing but her beating heart
to play the way, a different drum!
Crust peeled from the main,
silver flask filled with dreams
plucked from others minds.
Her own left town when she did.

Bella closes her eyes, awaits the sun
to shine upon her soiled gown,
while she whispers down the night.

Janet K. Brennan

Me and the Road, West

Casino stars light the sky
as I make my way west
along old route 66
.

A prayer to sweet Jesus
an old Texas Longhorn
does not decide
this be the night
to replace the missing
hood ornament
on my old Buick wagon
.

Icy hill yonder, glistens
white in the night,
 as I pump my brakes
An Eldorado in my rear view,
jump seat rising,
quick swerve to the left
Black ice making it so
tomorrow may not come.
Hell. . .
 the next exit may not come!
No guarantees in this life
.

Only me and the road, west
.

Ghosts rise from the side
Crosses, fake flowers
Someone died there
L.A. but a dream away
late for the icy drive
Hell, maybe not even a dream.
No guarantees in this life
.

Only me and the road, west

Doodles[2]

Packs on backs, they dash through halls,
white walls and hope.
Energy, bare heads and laughter .
.

Purpose!
.

Today she will fly,
and paint pictures from God.
Doodles on the wall, images on the ceiling,
newborn constellations
that have grown through the dark night. And when
the sun creeps from behind Watermelon Mountain,
.

a butterfly,
folding its wings
.

'pon the globe that gazes sweet reflections
through the garden of her life.
It prays a world –whole,
when beloveds push through the door,
Candy, kisses and packs on their backs; new slippers,
a poem from the elves left on her pillow
at home.
.

For tonight they will count dreams together, one on the bed,
one on the floor.
Whispering fairy stories...
.

Waiting.

_____

[2] This poem written for my granddaughter, Erin Elizabeth who was diagnosed
with Leukemia at age 5. She is now in remission.

Heart the Hunter

The city sleeps
She pulls her one-strapped gown
shoulders bare, beckoning
.

Sweet young men blinded
with lust and gin
dash cigars cold
in avenues- lonesome
never seeing her eyes
years of tears, swollen
legs mapped blue
low-hanging breasts, kissed worn
.

Sweet hunter in the night
Tomorrow she will eat
if tonight she does not die
...Welcome
A drink, a bed warm
to stave the morning chill
.

Eros- tango beneath sad lights
Crawling in random pattern
'Eat here'
She grasps
for another night of love
before the neon fades
for Heart the Hunter
.

Her neon fades

Janet K. Brennan

Royalty at Sweet Grass

High on the mountain he waited
for my gaze to meet his,
knowing we would be friends
should I stay my place above sweet- grass meadow.
.

Antlers twisted toward heaven,
copper velvet against turquoise,
he was the emperor north,
the king of the Sipapu;
conjurer of spirits.
None could dispute.
For some had tried, failed
when the quite gaze of humanity
slipped into his world, hoping
for the trophy.
.

My heart was not mine that day
as I turned toward camp.
How holy that place he stood!
Had he followed?
Pain rushed just before numb
as I dipped my feet into Rio Pueblo.
Sweet exhilaration!
Would I see him again?
Eyes serene, a saint upon the hill,
elegance in his stride,
while my own ached for the climb.
.

How I could have lingered under the solstice moon
to watch him dance!
But the sun hung low
as night crept upon my being,
my eyes could no longer bear the beauty of the day.

I felt him close, standing in the river,
watching me as I had watched him,
praying we became friends
that moment on the mountain
high above sweet- grass meadow,
when my gaze met his.

Janet K. Brennan

Life in Tangled Places
a Prayer for Joseph

Points of light, a half-million
meet stars of a universe-convoluted.
One ends, another begins.
False symmetry.
City songs, mingled with benzene
tug at my mind.
Graced by a single thought.
I am on terra firma,
yet alone.
And the world is not here.
It is there under the same moon where
Joseph lies in an empty cell, waiting.

Rose colored glasses.
I could use them!

Solitary in this tangled place.
As Joseph lies in the dark
where the floor meets the ceiling.
One ends, another begins.
False symmetry.
No points of light, only Luna
slipping through a two by four.
He is graced by a single thought.
He is alone.
The world is not here.
It is under the same moon where
she stands, waiting.

River Glass

Tables lean left
Cobblestones, unforgiving
at Cafe Michelle
~~
Le Pont Neuf, gently lit
reflects
as river glass on the Seine
Beaujolais tips the edge
spilling red on white linen
~~
They are here
Each night, the same
Elicit kisses, embraces secret
Perfume bold
mixed with passion' breath
Her leg slips over his
Bare breasts catch each heart beat
~~
He gently removes a leaf
from her tangled hair
They glance
Sweet intrusion, my soul lonely
As I raise my goblet
in pregnant salute

Momma's Souvenir

Rickety old rocker still keeps the beat
As it did forty years gone by
When the boys brought it home
From old route sixty-six,
Yet a neon glow in the sky

.

Old fry- bug- zappers cracked into the night
We had nothing but the land
And off on the highway, the old banjo picker
Played desert songs with his band

.

Down at Motel bar, the one on the left
With lanterns of Christmas gone by
We danced underneath them that New Year's Eve
While the boys shot them out, we got high

.

Belt souvenirs of the night, they said
When we drowned in Tequila and lime
A gift for you, Momma, to hang on your mirror
To always remember this time

.

When we danced til we fell
And we laughed til we cried
I took those old lights to be mine
They hang on my dresser, would they still light the night
If I only just took the time?

.

Rickety old rocker, a sent kiss from the past
Creaks with the memories gone by
When the boys brought it home from old route sixty-six
When the neon lit up the sky

Seshat; Anatomy of a Writer

There are days when her heart so heavy
it will not stay its place for the
uneven beat. She wonders,
what is this life?
Seshat, who laid awake counting stars.
For on the fifth sparkle, a wish fulfilled,
to know universal truths, what dream is that?
Did not Pegasus want a pony, Patricio a jump in the hay?
Dull, it is she who desires the secrets of heaven.
A wish perfect,
enlightenment, discovery,
leaping from star to star,
sprouting wings.
Each day searching, perhaps a bump,
an extra layer of skin
should her wish come true.
A wise man knows, how strange this world.
Pegasus got the hay jump.
Patricio got the pony.
Wings never sprouted.
And yet,
as her hands mapped, her face lined,
she knew
she could jump from star to star,
unlock the secrets of the Gods
with a dash of the pen.
The gift to the writer .
Can it lighten an old writer's heart,
or fulfill Seshat's wish?
.
Be sure...
as writers and artists, we paint pictures from God!

Janet K. Brennan

Sunrise Mountain
A Flight of the Soul

Needing each other
For I have gone to high places,
finding naught but Sweet-Briar
Yet, you have shown
that sweet briar heals
.

This flight with torn wings
above Sunrise Mountain
Kissing the crest, milk and honey
Sustenance for the one
Should I not return
.

I must return!
.

My pockets stuffed with dreams
Gathered from stars
Mine to claim
When I turn back.
.

 Oh, I must turn back!
.

Inhaling
This glorious light of flight
Mind without body
Transfiguration
Transportation to higher ground
And, what price or fear,
I carry for barter
Should I fly too high?
Yet, know in my journey

The choice is mine
When I go to the mountain
I may leave crumbs
To find my way home
For I will fly again
If I can come home

.

I must come home!

Janet K. Brennan

Swingin' on a Star

She sits in the corner, closet stark.
Those heels with the star,
rhinestones glow in the dark.
They bite at her toes,
her feet will look smaller.
Match the skirt tight,
she will look a bit taller.
Dimpled knees showing,
"Does it make me look fat?
Do I look all right?
Will they like me like that?"
.

A- in physics.
Life could be- guile.
The boy behind her,
in love with her smile.
He shared his A-,
a fool for her style.
He shares all his papers.
She 'll be smart for a while.
.

Soft voices in the kitchen.
Dishes crash to the floor.
"That's all right babe, I have plenty more.
You tried.'"
.

Mirror-gazing.
She kisses the glass.
Will they see her this time?
Will her dimpled knees pass?
A quick swig for courage.

She walks down the hall.
No time to be nervous.
Its them, after all.
.

Rhinestone star heels.
A fake A sets the mood.
Taller and smarter.
Will it make her look good?
Will they hold her and love her?
Will she be up to par?
'My darling, you are brilliant!'
Damn!

She should be swingin on a star!

Janet K. Brennan

Tête-à-Tête

Late lunch
We had to, you knew
Such arrogance
Crimes and misdemeanors
Your eyes blazed black
As you carved your mighty words
A table selected
Center stage-pleasant
Skyscrapers, streets busy below
Our little table
Always in the center
.

Equilibrium unmatched
Mine stolen
Sending me spinning off course
Yet, my turn to bask
Your secret and mine
Oh, dark sided moon
My secret, not yours

 I 've missed you. You must visit my flat
I ll call you, or you call me
When you are ready
I will never be ready
A sigh of relief, your panic room
My heart locked open
Yours gone missing
.

You look great.
You lie so well
.

And out comes the stop watch,
Center Table
We had to, you knew
Such arrogance
Sending me spinning off course
My turn

.

                    You always need the center

Janet K. Brennan

The Last Boat Home

Fading
Piazza San Marco
Behind clouds, grounded
My love affair strong,
for this tarnished gem
Blue striped, straw hat- tucked under my arm
Purchased on the Brenta
Signed by Byron, he never lived there

The Taxi awaits
Only that boy and me, steadies the tilt
A silent glide
Lamps half-lit reflect on the water
Minglers, feet splashing another time,
when Venice loved to love
Oh, how it loved to love!

Canals swallowing secrets of
God-like lust,
take from the trespass, souls spewed back
from watery graves

Tinkling sounds in the Veneto night

Mom, I heard wind chimes tonight
I know love, I heard them, too

Memories of swallowed secrets
take from the trespass, spewed back
Another place where I loved to love
Oh, how I loved to love!

Arriving, the boy smiles into my face
He jumps from the boat
And I wonder
Did he see my tears?

Janet K. Brennan

Abend's Blessing

We danced across moss-fur wrapped flowers,
Edelweiss.
Turning fields of gold- green to dotted Swiss gowns.
Covering alpine meadows, frenzied- Monet.
We climbed,
staffs held tightly through puddles half frozen.
The Zugspitz-mid fall, a grumpy old man,
chides us for losing our group two miles back.
Not a care should we fall to Abend's blessing
and spend the night under silent, white stars.
For life followed behind committing to dreams
we left in the foothills where first we began.

Oh, let us spend nights under silent, white stars!
.

When we saw her peeking o' re the next rise.
A princess abandoned by Monks and Wood Fairies.
Modest her steeple rose beneath oak.
Patiently waiting for chants and changes.
Doors left open, windows raised to the crisp.
She sighed gentle tales of mightier days.
.

For time was not in this high mountain place,
as we knelt in prayer and drank from our skins.
Like children we laughed when we found an old coin;
and cried when it fell through the cracks in the floor.
A call through the mountains, our friends are approaching,
happy to find us and rest for a while.
Then we quickly surrendered to Abend's Blessing.
The swift descent back through the Edel below.
 Where a fire waited beside our spun dreams.

With Pilsner and Snitznel and stories in Ehrwald.
We gazed the path back and knew we were blessed
in that high mountain chapel,
the princess of Abend
.

For life followed behind committing to dreams
we left in the foothills where first we began.
Oh, let us spend nights under silent, white stars!
God, let us spend nights under silent, white stars!

Shadows of Rhineland Phaltz, Alt Dahn

Valley ghosts,
lost in Alt Dahn woods.
Death has not conquered
this lover's soul!
Where misty morns creep castle walls.
Three sisters at Dahner locks,
mossy settlers waiting
the mid-day sun,
warm their barren flanks;
and pray for darkest night.
.

I wander
through gardens of wilde- rose
where the river ends,
and the valleys rise,
as does my heart at thought
of another enchantment
beneath this ancient sky,
my soulful comfort
laid bare in shadows.
.

I will write of this;
a lover's quill in Rhineland Phaltz.

Jungle-Bug Fires

You sit, the weight of the world,
they say; jungle-bug fires
etched glass, a forever stain
carved into your soul
while you breathe your war prayer.

Such shoulders stronger for the pain!

Yes, crossing the river wild took much
from your smile.
Furrowed brows that hide the scar.
A time of which you barely speak
save climbing that mountain, and
coming home with your dreams intact,
but your weeping is heard unto the night.

This you must do, as your father did.
Smiling your cry.
You cry,
and play your fiddle long into the night
erasing jungle-bug fires.
.

Pretending the world found peace.

Janet K. Brennan

For Brian; May You Always Dance[3]

Stopping by...
Book in hand. Will you sign it?
My God!
He has grown, a man.
Wife and children.
Seventeen years gone by.
.

The day she died,
he held her in his arms,
his first true love.
I peeked into his soul
as he whispered in her ear.
Dear Lord, he loved her so!
They cried.
.

Though she could not move,
one small tear, cradled
in the corner of her eye
blended with his
face pressed close.
Please don't go!
.

He disappeared that day.
We searched.
Unpacked bags, he left his mind
in that stark room,
placing it beside the note in her purse.
'How to please your man.'

---

[3] *This poem was written for Brian Swift. He was my deceased daughter, Kristen's, true love at athe time of her death at age 21. We lost track of Brian for many years following, but he has come back into our lives and gone full circle...for Brian*

He floated away on a dreamless sea.

I need closure.
Long years have taken their toll.
Traveled far but never left.
Yet, I have arrived !
Book in one hand, mine in the other,
he squeezed hard.
Will reading it hurt?
One small tear, cradled
in the corner of my eye
blended with his.

Dear Lord, we loved her so!
We cried!
.

For Brian.
 May You Always Dance!

Janet K. Brennan

Fred Astaire Fingers

Damn this line!
Longer than yesterday, late.
Neon blinks closing time.
Behind the counter, a robot.
She has no heart, I know.
It left town
when her husband did.
No heart
to bounce across the universe,
a ball, soaking in last nights tears.
No!
No heart-no tears!
.

A carved body in front .
Mutilated skin-yellow.
Black Crucifix peeps from shag.
A rose beneath purple hair,
licks his collar, frayed .
Metallica.
She smiles, bruising her lips,
as Fred Astair fingers dance
across dirty keys,
pretending not to notice
a back- pack stuffed.
.

Life on the run, babies to feed.
She sees it and nods,
eyes square as the register rings.
A pack of Cool Milds.
 Will that be it?
Yes, Ma' am, that's it.

He is gone, her lips bruise more
as she packs her beating heart
into her own satchel
buried beneath folds
on her well-worn sleeve.

Kids!

Janet K. Brennan

Giuseppe's Canzone'

Gatto Sophia sits.
She licks his whiskered chin.

He has fallen in his dreams;
sleeping in his days,
as grapes grow sweet
in his fields of vine grown fallow.
No cantina this year,
save the one where he sits
drinking grappa-soiled,

until the sun sets behind hills of neglect.
.

Beside the castle wall she lies.

Morning vespers waft, he mourns the morning,
singing that song, her favorite one,
placing flowers high
on marble engraved with tears.
.

      'I am not gone, just there.
      A whisper at the end of a prayer.
      Forget me now, the time will come.
      Our song of love once more we'll share.'
.

      He cries.
      'I can not find my life, my dear.
      The one I mis-placed just last year.
      I 've searched and yet can't seem to find.
      I 'll look again tonight, I swear!'
.

But he' ll drink this night
'neath an unseen moon,
praying he can forget.
Will she listen or see his barren field?
Wasting the night, a stink on his breath,
as the harvest waits for another year.
Pray, the harvest waits for another year!
.

Tomorrow will come, he will visit again,
placing flowers on marble-engraved.

    'I am not gone, just there.
    A whisper at the end of a prayer.
    Forget me now, the time will come.
    Our song of love once more we'll share.'
.

    He cries.
    'I can not find my life, my dear.
    The one I mis-placed just last year.
    I' 've searched and yet can't seem to find.
    I' ll look again tonight, I swear!'

Then he' ll sleep all day,
and sing through the night, la lirica grande'.

It was her favorite song.

Janet K. Brennan

Lamentation of an Aging Bride

And I ask myself.
Where were you when my flower
dripped with nectar sweet?
Destiny,
reveal it, oh sir!
Upon your horse white, and I
clad in my take me boots,
clinging to that myth
of Knights and Wizards fair,
hiding in my bejeweled lair.
.

Yet, here you are.
My dream invader.
As I offer no defense,
nor take umbrage.
Smiling unto my soul.
Sweet rain, a new beginning.
Moving to my place of comfort
among wildflowers and clover.
Oh!
Where were you when my eyes,
clear as healing pools,
imbibed that magic-wine?
Savoring
and soothing my heart' s dark night.
.

For now you come,
strumming your Midas harp,
placing flowers 'pon my limbs
mapped in colors faded-jaded.
A stooped flower, aging.

Petals dripping dew
in the morning sun
after a coldest night.
And I ask myself.
Where were you, sir,
when I flowed nectar-sweet?
And all the world was wrapped
in wreaths of myrtle pine .
As I clung to that myth
of Knights and Wizards, fair.

You were not there!

Janet K. Brennan

The Author

She sits by the pool,
behind shades of brown, yellow tints.
Book balanced on knees bronze.
Pages white with unwritten words,
as reality fades once the story begins.
.

Orchestration perfect, accepting
only the Caribbean breeze,
inhaling valleys of salt entrails
carved beneath her eyes.
Curtain call, she needs the play.
.

Her fingers bleed
from the shell buried within her hand.
Life's grace held, now gone,
lost in ravaging of turbulent seas.
Crystal-bowl destined!
.

She looks into the soul
of the old lady reading near her;
turning the pages, looking for more
as she sits by the pool
behind shades of brown, yellow tints.
.

'Do you like that book? I am the author.'

Adio di Montecchia

~~~Montecchia
falls behind while I,
in valley, deep
am not eager to be gone.

Temptress, enshrouded
in veils of morning wizardry.
Pearls of gray mist
swirl a siren's dance
as I turn toward home.

~~~Seductress,
me within her fold
of hillside green,
tended my broken wing,
made love to my soul
...her fruit rich.
I bathed in her juices,
slave-rendered
to her Midas sunset.

A gentle hold
upon my tired spirit,
stronger with each farewell.
Releases her grasp.
I have sung my last
as I turn toward home.

~~~

Janet K. Brennan

Misty Morn on Old Gray Pond

Winter fire burns
stoked with pinion cones
welcoming me to this day.
Remembering, quick prayers sighed
before falling to dreams.
A promise whispered through the night
that with the sun-rising
the world finds peace.
.

As light peeps through window-frost,
I can not sleep
for the gathering birds,
as choirs of seraphim singing
on Old Gray Pond.
.

Stepping into the misty morn,
still water reflects mountains
painted white,
leaning close, inhaling
peace of God's lake shrine.
.

Distant Loons call through reeds,
announce the day
for lion and lamb to embrace.
Sustenance divine, this place
to soothe those wounded souls
in a battle lost and a world undone.

.

Holy day on old Gray Pond.
For all to bathe in healing mists
and revel in the knowledge;
peace begets peace and we are one.
A new beginning,
.

Is this a dream?
Or am I first to take a place
along the misty shore?
.

If I reach and touch another,
and they the same, I will know.
.

Hands entwined with hands,
warm embraces filled with love
whisper in the wind the truth.
.

This is the day the world begins,
this misty morn on old Gray Pond.

Janet K. Brennan

Memories of Dinner on the Adige'

Sumptuous dinner, late.
Ingesting what I recognized,
French cognac, watered down.
. . .One more chapter.
.

Sliding the case, golden .
Secretly inhaling contents
of old tobacco spice, long gone.
. . .I miss it!
'

Ducks in a half-filled moat
slide down crevices, antique
in this city by the Adige.
Castelvecchio, moss covered,
beckons in the dank, river- night,
. . .gathered treasures.
.

That last amber swig,
fiery hidden vice, rendering
me vulnerable to cobblestones
that separate me from my hotel.
.

A rumbling autobus.
Companions smoke and dust,
drown out the edge
of my last drink.
'

"Lira for my sick child, Signora?"
Aspirin in my pockets,
impatience on my breath.
Forgotten gratuities, placed
into her hand, trembling.
.

Domani, I will move on!

Janet K. Brennan

Fair Valley

O! When comes the end?
Brown on crackle-brown
as east wind whispers trails,
frost- biting canyon walls
and settling upon tired limbs.
Whirly gigs, weed tumbling
catch upon my gate, mock flowers,
my garden dry and thorny.
.

Where are the Sage Grouse?
Fair weather friends they be!
I thought they sang last night.
T'was only the hooting of the wind,
and dry embers waiting for wood,
promising no change;
nor quick respite.
.

I walked yesterday,
burying my face in wool,
laughing at chill that crept through the weave,
leaving its mark long after
my return to the blaze.
Finally warming my face,
melting my heart for a purpose greater.
.

Winter in this desert high, chilling.
Seems to last forever.
For my mind has forgotten its verdant,
Fair Valley
that will fall to the surface
with the last cold blow.

In Equation; At Best

Life in spurts-random, at best.
A heart weary for anything more. Words
smolder on tired lips, true and yet scorch
as hell's fire.
She was good for you; yet brought out
the worst when at her best.

No bitter sweet taste in this sad goodbye.
For the tongue can not savor
what it never tasted.
Life in spurts-random, in equation

at best.

Janet K. Brennan

Odds and Ends at Sipapu Creek

The sweet gentle sound of a rhyming wind
whispers down Sipapu Creek.
A whirlwind snow and spitting rain,
spinning trees to glass .
White-faced rocks
pocked with dirt, eyes errantly peeking
toward Beaver Ridge Dam .
Splintered memories
of when the creek did flow.
.

Trickles of water.
A trail for climbing; ruts perfect
for soft, summer feet.
Now frozen in early day cold.
I search for what was lost,
caught in the bramble.
My heart in pieces, strewn.
Odds and ends.
As we jumped into the mossy deep
to cool in Sipapu Creek.
.

Our rock, special, now cracked with cold,
snow covered in pine- sap ice.
We kissed.
As the gentle sighs of a rhyming wind
carried us beyond the creek and into the wild
of our own desire.
Another time and season,
when the creek did flow and the sweet rhyming wind
sighed down a roaring creak,
merging its destiny with ours.

Leaving naught but odds and ends
in the early day cold.
Inhaling that time
when the creek did flow
and life was warm at Sipapu .

Janet K. Brennan

Praying for the Heart of Ossa[4]

She left on Sunday morn
as I burned eggs.
We never heard her leave,
nor the squeak
of the tired screen door;
that rainy day in June,
though the raven quorked
her name, Ossa.
.

I heard its wings
battling my window pane,
a whirligig black
losing control in a wind-war
that fell down from the north.
It scattered her dreams
alongside bible pages
she burned the night before.
.

I would have said good-bye!
.

Stained fingers
slipped through holes
in my tired jean pockets,
caressing the cross she gave me,
buried in sandy corners;
caught in threads.
Upside-down, a devils omen.
.

---

[4] *Ossa is the Greek Goddess of gossip and slander*

She smiled a crafty game
of trust and innocence.
A tabernacle etched in rose glass,
spreading prisms of light
that darkened as her steps grew cold.
And no one knew the truth;
not even she.
Ossa left on a Sunday morn
while I burned eggs
and prayed for her heart.
.

I should have said good-bye!
.

.

.

Janet K. Brennan

Rose in My Hair: a New England Reverie

White picket fence
leaning low to the ground
Welcomes me home
heaven-bound
.

Down the lane
where ocean meets sky
I've been away
No answers to why
.

Surf against rocks
of misty pearl gray
Keeps beat with my heart
on this glorious day
.

My mail box empty
save leftover vines
Reminding me now
of happier times
.

A dried red rose
in the window- bay
Picked lone side the road
on that very last day
.

When he stroked it so gently
the color of wine
Then placed in my hair
his full lips on mine
.

The cottage now empty
seduces my heart
Throw open the widows
a brand new start!
.

Tomorrow he'll come
with his children and wife
Sweet refrains
from another life
.

My small twin bed
nestled under the eaves
A crackling fire
stoked with crispy fall leaves

As I curl up to sleep
and shed every care
I am home in New England
with a rose in my hair

Janet K. Brennan

Salome's Wisdom

High on the mountain, she knew.

As the wind blew south,
her life shifting,
as veils from Salome's Dance.

One by one she hailed
her nakedness, flesh fired as saffron
thrown cold in the morning sky.
Twirling in wisdom- mist,
a truth revealed.
Each time showing
more than she could change;
changing more than she could grasp.

Her past, a wilted primrose
falling to her feet,
tinting them blue.
.
Truth was not!
.
As she tumbled forth
while he tried
to hold her steady;
for him, not her.
And who would know
but saving grace
or the mountain birds
who carried her veils unto the peak?

As she bade farewell

to the silken threads she knew.
A brief disguise. . .
For underneath the veils,
Salome danced

She was always there!

Janet K. Brennan

Nesting Hats and Worn Slippers

Summer came, went like a flash .
Soft scents of wet grass -old hats.
Weathered slippers nesting on the porch,
collecting scents of memories left behind .
A family waits.
She called, whispering through breath hollow.
A calloused voice, not the first time, not the last.

.

He is ill; he may not see tomorrow-baby can'tt breathe.
A good family gathers, offers healing thoughts, prays
for a late summer breeze to come
and sweep the porch clean, scattering nesting hats
and worn slippers -gone forever in the wind.
Pray, shatter the lie- life holds only one good tear.
The promise that only one bloom will fall from the vine
or carry sharp thorns to pierce a mother's heart.

.

Come alone, leave alone!

.

Tis the middle journey cared and shared.
Pray, a good family has strength, love
to carry through nesting slippers and weathered hats
left out on the porch,
long gone from late summer' s blow.
Yet, collect scents of memories left behind,
when summer came and went like a flash,
and a family gathered to pray.

Nova Love

Free-fall, pain swift.
      She' d felt the ground before.
           The death of a dream stains the heart,
             and strains the soul.

.

Sweet star!

.

More brilliant than the rest.
Close enough to kiss.
Far enough to hide.
Hot enough to burn.
Fast enough to flee.
Her hands, burdened-sore.

.

Ripped open for the climb.
Everyone searches, few ever find.
Faltering.
Hurling to depths.
Unsaved by that magic net.
Where was the net?

.

      A wind dusting, please!

.

And a softer tomorrow
should she fall once more.
Craving that shine,
the beacon that will blind her
to the reality that perhaps
it never existed at all.

Janet K. Brennan

Terza Rima: The Riddle of Dante and Milton

Pray, tell me on what circle
through the book of prose?
Deep I go, deeper yet.
Finding naught but pieces,
wood charred by the side.
Carvings hacked within its core,
marks the way.
A key on the ground.
Its riddle,
life.
Its answer,
existence.
Should I climb those steps, a perfect count?
Oh!
What lay behind that lofty door?
Divine in its complexity.
And yet a cut tree,
giving many splinters.
This mystery, the answer moaned
by winds that call my name.
A puzzle worth fitting, forgotten.
The answer?
Did I bring it with me when I came,
or lose it when I fell from grace?
Through first circle to fifth.
Sweet metaphor of life.
Purgatory.
.

Oh life what story can you bring?
The Answer is not mine to know!
Purgatory on the very first ring.

.

Oh life I wander helpless soul!
With key in hand, steps in my count,
solving the mystery, Paradise my goal.

Janet K. Brennan

Pax: Vines on the Hill

My dream of peace

Standing there, this wizard, crown broken
by falls from his holy- high place.
Scars gorged deep into his chest
from his imminent fall from grace.
.

For life leaves its deep and tender mark
where the armor does not fold.
And knowing when to stand aside
is worth its price in gold.
.

Come fly with me, Pax!
Our hopes will build dreams.
Your joy feeds my hungry soul .
Finally harmony.
At last we break bread.
War has ended and taken its toll.
.

As we spread our wings,
entwine fingers as vines
on an arbor of sweet- lilly- white.
Incantations, creation of life and love.
Embracing a world filled with light.
.

For strength will grow
with our lighter load
upon broad wings that will not fold.
Beneath the weight of killing fields
entrust with a harness of gold.
.

He placed in my hands an olive branch.
Snapped by the last fiery round.
Upon my head a three ringed wreath,
made of willow from fallow ground.
.

It will drop its seeds and spread with the wind,
with care from a helping hand.
This new olive branch made of slow fired souls
will spread its glow 'round the land.
.

We have waited forever, my wizard, O dove.
A promise when all said and done.
What we knew in our hearts could only be found
once our vines on the hill joined as one.
.

Standing there, this wizard, crown bent
by falls from his holy- high place.
Scars gorged deep into his chest
by his imminent fall from grace.
.

For life leaves its deep and tender mark.
When everything' s said and done.
What we knew in our hearts could only be found,
once our vines on the hill joined as one.

_____

* Janet K. Brennan

To Say Goodbye

Net in hand she ran
I want him Gram
Into a tiny box, he will go
I will watch him grow
I love him so!
.

I can not catch him, Gram
He spreads his wings
High unto the sky
I want him so!
.

I caught him Gram
See how his wings
fold in prayer?
Sweet colors of the rainbow
Oh think how he once crawled
upon the ground
Now he flies!
.

He does not fly, my dear
He has not room to spread his wings
Tiny feet now scratch
Fluttering about, vain attempts
A cell for his effort
He can but pray
for a kind heart
who will set him free
That he may kiss the sky
once more
.

I need him Gram,

I will cry should he die
His home beneath your gazing globe
See how he watches,
bowing in surrender
Yet should I lift the lid,
will he leave forever?

.

His freedom is my offer
should he remain
in his box with holes
I will know
Here is where he wants to be

.

There Gram, see his tender wings
So lovely, watch him fly
Goodbye
Watch him fly. . . good-bye!

Janet K. Brennan

Shangri-La

Sitting in the back, she watched.
Farewells, flowers and candles.
Smiles of joy, tears of sadness.
The caged.
The outside looking in.
Emotions caught in cogs
that spun 'round and 'round
going no where.
As she patted her belly-swollen.
Proud of her body morphing
to something everyone hated.
.

Bus fumes choked her dreams
of Shangri-la,
and places of the heart where everyone cared.
No timpani needed,
she was her own parade.

Sore in the pruning, wings clipped.
Wrapped tightly around her heart.
Shattered, bleeding.
Pressing her nose against a window-dirty
dotted with beads of rain,
veins of life,
she watched the world go by
in slow motion; the same song
going 'round and 'round
in her tired mind
like cogs in a wheel.

As she traveled at the speed of light
toward nothing.

Pondering the Unseen State of Being

ashen tomorrows, we sail upon a sea
of latent prophetic spews, angry metaphor
as evolution takes its toll cramping nature
confined into hazy mists
of new colors that bathe disappearing hands
and scorch hermetic souls
.

leaflets-tender green, fallow upon the ground
blow away in a chemical dust

leaving trails of verdant
morphed bodies, slowly on the rise
the unseen state of being
hailing nightmares, self-proclaimed
survival without flesh the last option
.

tell me, where came this hell

was anybody raptured

can we forget tomorrow-ashen
and return to yesterday

Janet K. Brennan

Strip Tease

Another night upon her bed of nails
Stripped-sweet penance
Fingers sore, hands swollen
from grasping old transgressions;
those she buried deep beneath the unravel
of weathered weave
And yet they peep through threads bare,
tripping her as she dances
.

They will not stay their place!
.

Though hidden well yet ill conceived,
should they ever see the light of day
She ties another knot into its braid
and swears by the light of a half swung moon
that she never meant to hurt

Freuline Perfect

Train rails weathered
through a muddy pass
on this old track of mountain
the way to Zermatt.
Lake Crystal, white-blue,
icy under a sun melting snow,
sends puffs of mist into the
late summer day.
Mother- mountain.
Forever clouds hide its face,
waiting for the Freuline perfect.

Sie morgan mich?
You like me?

She slips beneath feathered down
to walk through the streets.
Strudel and coffee with creme, Elsie's Place.
Resting on a splintered bench,
camera in hand
as the mountain smiles down on the village.

Sleeping, Matterhorn,
removes its mask.
Reveals its peak.

It has found the perfect Freuline!

Janet K. Brennan

The Hundred Year

The screen door creaked.
Old Seb' s nose pressed nigh.
Its comin... rumblin
from Blood Mountain high!
.

That whistle stop roar
put fear in us all.
Rain, lightning,
 a thick black wall.
.

Like a derailed train
from old Silver Pass.
It is coming again,
just like the last.
..

It cut 'cross the desert;
hide or keep high.
No longer in Oz.
Yet we' re ready to fly.
.

A second hundred year
that summer past.
The third since Trube house
washed in a flash.
..

Just mud and rock
from yonder high.
Roaring mighty, she hit
in the blink of an eye.
..

Not a warning came,
save old Seb' s nose
pressed hard to the screen.
We knew it was close.
..
The gal in the foothills,
her car washed down.
Arroyo Embudo,
Spun 'round and 'round.
.
Leaving no trace
'cept the jump seat rear.
Stickin' out of the mud
in that hundred flood year.
.
Took her soul that day .
It almost took mine.
We lost all we had.
Not a penny to shine!
.
That whistle-stop roar
put fear in us all.
Rain, lightning,
a thick black wall.
.
Like a runaway train
from Old Silver Pass.
It will come again,
Damn sure won t be the last!

Janet K. Brennan

Girl's Night Out

On the mesa, walking,
as night descends.
My boots,
turned with the stain
of life.
My skirt on a coat-wire
for the burning.
I wait~~

For the show of
heaven -sent glow.
One with the city below.
A star gaze, I know!

Night winds hawk
my face.
Carry my soul with them
'cross the valley
to the Rio Grande.
Rise to the mountain, Sandia.

Match in my pocket,
hand -dusting my boots,
I wonder~
How did I come to be
in this place of glory,
under the desert sky ...
a long way from home,

if not for God?

One

As we raise our hands on high,
we kiss our blessed soil.
For though the mountain meets the sky,
the climb is worth the toil.

A peace has fallen over the world,
a gentle hush of grace.
And in the pre-dawn afterglow,
a sweet and smiling face.

Our hands we clasp in layered hues.
We know our prayers are heard.
A whisper soft and e' re subdued,
as winds of change are stirred.

We know that something great has turned.
Our hopes have come alive.
Too many years we all have yearned.
Together now we strive.

Brave smiles, the tears of joy abound
to wash away the stain.
Not much to lose this time around,
and oh so much to gain!

And as we raise our hands on high,
life spills down glory path.
Arms entwined, collective sigh.
Our spirits one-at last!

Our spirits one at last!!!!

In hopes for our new President, Barrack Obama

Janet K. Brennan

The Girl on Beach

Sand-chair, rusted
Tucked under her arm
Beach bag, bursting
with beer cans empty
tin against tin
Her long legs tanned
disappearing into powder
Muscles sore from too many hikes
along the red-tide shore
She laughs at golden hues
seen only by her
above the horizon, beyond her grasp
Reaching for them yesterday
Rays slipped through her fingers
and into the sea
She will get them tomorrow
Popping open another beer
swigging, dreaming
that it is champagne
Hell, she hated champagne
Who is that lady
in the swim suit, yellow
The one who tiptoes to the shore
Measuring her own shadow
against those around her
Maybe she can tell her. . .
Should she move to Georgia?

Two Candles

Tell me, was I not?
Her name you whispered
through hair, perfumed
with candles by your bed,
wafting scents of jasmine.
My funniest story-you laughed
yet touched another's face
in the waning hours of desire.

Bare shoulders hurt for carrying
the weight of your sorrow.

Feet bleeding for walking in your boots.
Mirrored reflections, not my face
but hers as it became mine.

My lips singed with your passion-flame,
yet your heart lies cold, only
two candles melting
by your bed.
Oh, was I not?

Woven Threads

Sure as a Nightingale
sings for no one

Youth gone, I cannot
dance amongst
wildflowers, purple stretched
in fields of forever

No eyes to gaze across
tangerine hints of sunset

Woven threads of a golden life,
pass quickly,

yet stir a fire,
nothing missed

Flying through destiny.
Wings, gilded
Loving all that is
Accepting all that is not
of woven threads.

*For my mother whom has been afflicted with macular degeneration
and is 91 years young!*

A Winter Bloom

Petals . . . soft
I wonder just how
For deep winter frost
now hangs from its brow

Scent, sweet tender
Getting stronger each year
"Look at me now,
for I am yet here!"

Deep winter bloom
Put to the test
Delicate blends
A Rose at its best!

Janet K. Brennan

Jude's Trip[5]

You came to me in my dream- trip.
Lilac scents filled my room
darkened by grief .

Mercy! No more, please.

Can you remember?
Pain, yours shared-mine lost in the effort
of always joining in your tarantella.
Sweeping those spiders under a mat of legacy,
yours, not mine.
When you fell that time, bruised
by those mad demons- reaching
thorns sharp, slicing each time.
My hand calloused.

You waved goodbye, sighing.
I am not for this world, another waits
in the darkness beyond the last star.
And you may not follow,
for this trip is mine, alone;
but I will remember.

Oh, will you peek into my journey and
send me wildflowers in my dreams?
For I am lost in my tarantella!
Sweeping those spiders, lest they poison
their dance of dances.

Will you remember?

---

[5] This poem written for one of my dearest friends, Jude Downey, who passed
away in the spring of 2009

This Place

This place,
seen, not remembered
beckons through patches
of eternity.

> Across fields of forever,
> to a garden unknown
> Calls us to task
> in mortal surrender
> of the temporary.

> Knowing . . .
> before we arrived
> that we would find
> treasures. . .
> spiritual bounties
> to share.

> In this place
> across the stars
> once seen, not remembered;
> a heavenly sojourn.

A leap of faith
through patches of eternity
to this place.

Janet K. Brennan

Windows

On the lake, night birds gather.

Old Long John, one foot missing,
waits,
then joins in reverie-sacred
for the man gone; the one who sat by the window
tapping, nodding.
Show me your wings.
Drift through citrine stars;
dip the water, black!
Pay homage to nightingale
who sings alone, yet waits
on the far edge,
his feathers perfect for the man
who tapped and nodded
on a summer night, warm

on the lake where night-birds gather.

~~~

In I loving memory of my father, Joseph F. Devan who passed through his window on the 5th of August, 2009. I love you, Dad.

I Think I Know

I cannot see my hands before me.
Please . . . is this a body?
Why can't I fly free?
I am so tiny, yet feel so big.
How will I manage to maneuver
this cumbersome vehicle
through this new life?
What is that sweet scent of angel dust?
Who is cuddling me in her arms,
is that my mother?

Why am I a seraph here?
Who am I now . . . really?
Where was I before?
Please, God . . . where am I going?
~~~I think I know!

I cannot see my hands before me.
I am old now,they shake.
Why do I yet have this body?
I wish I could fly free!
I am large now, yet feel so small.
Is that the scent of rose water?
Who is cuddling me so lovingly?
Is that my daughter?
I think I know!

Janet K. Brennan

Pray, Gently Pass the Night

Oh, were it that I could not feel
my heart bleeding, pierced by arrows
aimed perfectly, target bare.
My first born,
I never said good-bye.

Pray, gently pass the night!

Mend this soul, ripped to shreds,
for without I am emptied,
desiring nothing
but her presence, as we dance
in Your mansion of many rooms.
No pain . . .
should a child die first.

Pray, gently pass the night!

Wake me to a different morn.'
Oh! Was it but a dream?
For I will love her better, this day.
Or will she love me better, Your way?
She was never mine to keep, I know,
a precious gift, my Lamb, You know!

Treasure Chest

We gathered, tears between smiles
Laughter punctuated, the last margarita
One too many and not enough

Hands entwined; a prayer for him
The horizon dims
with one last swim, and a wave goodbye
 to a half-drowned sun
and a man we love
We are beyond the buoys,
remembering
treasures in a chest, scattered, given

Wanting only the moment

A tip of my hat, thumbs up
as the diva-red dips into the deep
Shark-bait in the gulf
off Siesta Key-old
thoughtful of why we can't spend the night
floating and dreaming
A family together

'It does not get any better than this!'

Janet K. Brennan

Finale

The lake beautiful!
 Pin-point sparkles of wave dotted with lace
Islands green in the distance,
as lily pads on Grace Pond.
They grow smaller; the song of the loons
more distant.
What a lovely place, this world
of desert, mountain and sea!
Its tutorial perfect, a lesson complete.
Love- challenges smaller than the last,
hills easier to climb.

Oh when did I learn to fly higher
than the closest star?

As the world below fades-azure,
this life, a celebration
in ritual, a journey through time,
 as blue turns to gold, then pearl.

Gentle tugs!

I have felt them before, those glorious hands.
They once opened and set a butterfly free in a garden of choice.
And now, once again beckon my soul.
As the lake sparkles gently, and islands grow larger.
Lake birds in choir, lily pads now islands.
With one final breath, a quick leap of faith,
and I am home!

Index

About Janet K. Brennan

Janet K. Brennan, AKA JB Stillwater, lives in the foothills of the Sandia Mountains in Albuquerque, New Mexico with her husband, Arthur, a great gray cat named Amos, and a border collie named JoJo.

Janet released a book of inspirational poetry entitled *A Stronger Grace* (Casa de Snapdragon, 2007), a book of southwestern poetry entitled *Recollections of an Old Mind, West* (Cyberwit Publishing, 2006), an historical novel entitled *Harriet Murphy: A Little Bit of Something* (Casa de Snapdragon, 2009) and a memoir taking a deep look inside herself entitled *A Dance in the Woods* (Casa de Snapdragon, 2007.)

Her poetry and short stories can be seen in various books and magazines, including: *SP Quill Magazine, Common Swords Magazine, The Power of Prayerful Living* (Rodale Books), *Taj Mahal Review* (Cyberwit), Different Worlds - A Virtual Journey (Cyberwit, 2006), *Chicken Soup for the Christmas Soul* (Chicken Soup for the Soul Publishing, 2008), and *Earthships, a New Mecca - An Anthology of New Mexican Writers* (Horse & Tiger Press, 2007.)

Her colored pencil art-work and photography have been published in *Taj Mahal Review* (Cyberwit, 2006) and she is currently writing book reviews which have been published in the Greenwich Village Gazette and can be viewed at her website jbstillwater.com.

Janet's on-line publications include Strangeroad.com as well as IdentityTheory.com where you can read her short stories, poetry and philosophical essays, including Existentialism; a Myopic View. She was the featured poet in Poetry Magazine in the autumn of 2007.

Janet attended the University of New Hampshire, Hesser Business College and has a legal certification from the University of New Mexico.

About Peggie Devan

Peggie Devan has been a Registered Nurse since 1970. She graduated from New England College in the state of New Hampshire in 1985 with a Bachelor of Science Degree with a dual major in Psychology/Sociology. During the first 15 years of her career she worked in various Intensive Care Units: Medical/Surgical, Pediatric, Coronary Care, Recovery Room and Cardio-thoracic Open Heart Units. The following 15 years were spent in the Department of Medicine as a Clinical Administrator to the Chief of Staff. Upon early retirement in 2000, Peggie moved to Sarasota, Florida and worked as a nurse at the Van Wezel Performing Arts Center. Her *Early Bloomer* childrens books were written as a gift for her niece, Erin, who was stricken with Leukemia.

Peggie's first published poem was entered into a contest to win back stage passes to meet her favorite musician, singer Josh Groban. She not only won the contest but received a phone call from Josh telling her that she had won the contest! This poem was written in Irish brogue and is entitled *Driven' Ta' Distruction O're The Singin' O' Me Josh*.

Two of Peggie's poems are featured in the novel *Harriet Murphy: A Little Bit of Something*. She is a guest author on the JB Stillwater, Inc. Literary Magazine where her touching family traditions poetry is read and enjoyed by viewers around the globe.

About Charles Adés Fishman

Charles Adés Fishman is Emeritus Distinguished Professor of English & Humanities at Farmingdale State College, where he created the Visiting Writers Program in 1979 and the Distinguished Speakers Program in 2001. He was series editor of the Water Mark Poets of North America Book Award and has served as poetry editor or guest editor for a wide range of publications, among them *Cistercian Studies Quarterly*, *Gaia*, *Journal of Genocide Research*, *New Works Review*, *Pedestal Magazine*, *PRISM: An Interdisciplinary Journal for Holocaust Educators*, and *Shirim*; he has also served as associate editor of *The Drunken Boat* and poetry consultant to the U.S. Holocaust Memorial Museum in Washington, DC. In 1995, Dr. Fishman received a fellowship in poetry from the New York Foundation for the Arts and in 2006, he was honored as "Long Island Poet of the Year" by the Walt Whitman Birthplace Association. His previous books include *Blood to Remember: American Poets on the Holocaust* (2007) and *Chopin's Piano* (2006), both from Time Being Books; *Country of Memory* (Uccelli Press, 2004); and *The Death Mazurka*, a 1989 American Library Association "Outstanding Book of the Year" that was nominated for the 1990 Pulitzer Prize in poetry. *Chopin's Piano* received the 2007 Paterson Award for Literary Excellence.

About Janet Yaeger

Janet Yaeger lives with her husband in southern Illinois. She writes poetry about real life situations and considers herself part poet, part story teller. Janet is a guest poet on the J.B. Stillwater poetry site. She is a regular contributor at The Poet Sanctuary, an on-line poetry site, where she holds the title of co-administrator. She has been published in "Splash of Verse: Volume 7", a Poet Sanctuary publication and was one of the featured poets from that site interviewed for Poetize Magazine, Volume One, September 2009, where she was also one of four first place winners of an art contest. She has also been published in a regional periodical, "The Country Register." Janet has won several awards for her poetry on the Poet Sanctuary site.

.

Recent Releases from Casa de Snapdragon

Water under Water
Charles Adés Fishman
Available in Paperback,
and eBook

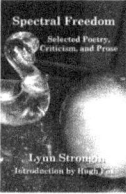

The Making of Tibias Ivory
Through the Eyes of Innocence
D. Allen Jenkins
Available in Paperback,
Hardcover, and eBook

Spectral Freedom
*Selected Poetry, Criticism,
and Prose*
Lynn Strongin
Available in Paperback,
Hardcover, and eBook

A Scattering of Imperfections
Katrina K Guarascio
Available in Paperback,
Hardcover, and eBook

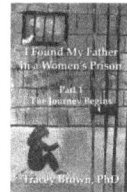

The Poetry Café
John Newlin
Available in Paperback
and Hardcover

**I Found My Father in a
Women's Prison**
Tracey Brown, PhD
Available in Paperback and
Hardcover

Harriet Murphy
A Little Bit of Something
Janet K. Brennan
Available in Paperback,
Hardcover, and eBook

A Stronger Grace
Janet K. Brennan
Available in Paperback

**Recollections of an Old
Mind, West**
Janet K. Brennan
Available in Paperback

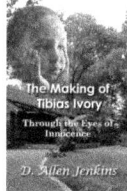

Be sure to visit us at **https://www.casadesnapdragon.com** for
purchasing information on these and other fine books by Casa
de Snapdragon Publishing

NOTES